For Casey McCarthy—D.D.M.

To my mom and dad.—J.D.

© 2005 Dandi Daley Mackall.

© 2005 Standard Publishing, Cincinnati, Ohio.

A division of Standex International Corporation.

All rights reserved. Printed in China.

Project editor: Robin Stanley.

Cover and interior design: Marissa Bowers.

Scripture quotations are taken from The Holy Bible, New Living Translation, copyright © 1996.

Used by permission of Tyndale House Publishers, Inc., Wheaton, IL. 60189.

All rights reserved.

12 11 10 09 08 07 06 05   9 8 7 6 5 4 3 2 1

Library of Congress Cataloging-in-Publication Data

Mackall, Dandi Daley.

I'm his lamb / written by Dandi Daley Mackall ; pictures by Jane Dippold.

p. cm. -- (My favorite verses)

ISBN 0-7847-1533-5 (case bound picture book)

1. Bible. O.T. Psalms XXIII--Paraphrases, English--Juvenile literature.

I. Dippold, Jane. II. Title. III. Series: Mackall, Dandi Daley. My Favorite verses.

BS145023rd .M23 2005   223'.20520834--dc22   2004017953

God is my shepherd and
I'M HIS LAMB

Written by Dandi Daley Mackall   Pictures by Jane Dippold

STANDARD PUBLISHING
CINCINNATI, OHIO

Hey, everybody! Know who I am?

God's my shepherd.
I'm his lamb.

What if it stops raining

and the rivers all go dry?

What if crops quit growing

and the farmers don't know why?

What if stores are empty

and there's nothing left to buy?

I'll never worry. God meets my needs.

He makes the raindrops, and he grows the seeds!

The LORD is my shepherd; I have everything I need.

Psalm 23:1

Whenever there's no room for me
to sit on Mommy's lap,
I fall into a fussy, cranky, crabby, kind of trap.
But I'm okay if I just pray . . .
and maybe take a nap.

Then I remember who I am.

God's my shepherd.
I'm his lamb.

He lets me rest in green meadows.
Psalm 23:2

People get so busy,
and they rush from here to there.

Hurry! Scurry! Makes me worry,
running everywhere.
But I can find a quiet spot.
I sneak away in prayer . . .

Whispering, "Jesus, here I am!"

You're my shepherd.
I'm your lamb.

He leads me beside peaceful streams.

Psalm 23:2

I can run, and jump, and dive,
and tumble, throw, and kick!
But even I get tired,
or I might get hurt or sick.
Yet when I turn to Jesus, I feel better mighty quick!

God has made me like I am.

He's my shepherd.
I'm his lamb.

He renews my strength.   Psalm 23:3

I could take so many roads. I know there's lots at stake.

For one path is the right path, and the other ones are fake.

But with the Bible as my map,

I'll know which road to take . . .

For on God's path is where I am.

God's my shepherd.
I'm his lamb.

He guides me along right paths, bringing honor to his name.

Psalm 23:3

Sometimes I get frightened,
and I lie awake at night.
With lightning flashing,
thunder crashing,
nothing feels all right.

But I know God's beside me,
and he turns the dark to light . . .

'Cause God is everywhere I am!

He's my shepherd.
I'm his lamb.

What if I am playing, and a bully comes my way?
I'm much too small to fight him off,
if he won't let me play.
But God is so much bigger!
I will always be okay.

And all will see whose kid I am!

God's my shepherd.
I'm his lamb.

Your rod and your staff protect and comfort me.
Psalm 23:4

If a guy makes fun of me,
"Hey, buddy, you're too slow!"
He takes my cookie, leaves me none,
and shouts, "Get out, now! Go!"
But God prepares a feast for me,
and soon that guy will know . . .

Jesus loves me like I am.

God's my shepherd.
I'm his lamb.

You prepare a feast for me in the presence of my enemies.
Psalm 23:5

Cats and dogs and polliwogs,
father, sister, mother,
Grandpa, Grandma, all my friends,
even little brother—
blessings, blessings everywhere!

And now, here comes another . . .

Who's a blessing? Hey! I am!

God's my shepherd.
I'm his lamb.

You welcome me as a guest, anointing my head with oil.
My cup overflows with blessings.

Psalm 23:5

What if, when I'm bigger, I forget the God I know?
Will he come and find me,
keep on searching high and low?
Yes! Even when I'm all grown up,
my God won't let me go!

God will know just where I am.

He's my shepherd.
I'm his lamb.

Surely your goodness and unfailing love will pursue me all the days of my life.
Psalm 23:6

From now on and for all time,
because of Jesus' grace,
I'll have heaven for my home,
'cause God saves me a place!
Living with my shepherd, I can love him face to face.

I'll be with the great I AM!

He's my shepherd.
I'm his lamb.

And I will live in the house of the LORD forever.

Psalm 23:6

Psalm 23

The LORD is my shepherd;
I have everything I need.
He lets me rest in green meadows;
he leads me beside peaceful streams.
He renews my strength.
He guides me along right paths,
bringing honor to his name.

Even when I walk
through the dark valley of death,
I will not be afraid,
for you are close beside me.
Your rod and your staff
protect and comfort me.

You prepare a feast for me
in the presence of my enemies.
You welcome me as a guest,
anointing my head with oil.
My cup overflows with blessings.

Surely your goodness and unfailing love
will pursue me
all the days of my life,
and I will live in the house of the LORD
forever.